Fairy Wishes
for Friends

*Fairy Wishes for Friends: A Pocket Treasure Book
of Friendly Thoughts*

Illustrations copyright © 2005 by Becky Kelly Studio LLC

Text copyright © 2006 by River House Media, Inc.

For information write Andrews McMeel Publishing,
an Andrews McMeel Universal company,
4520 Main Street, Kansas City, Missouri 64111.

06 07 08 09 10 EPB 10 9 8 7 6 5 4 3 2 1

ISBN-13: 978-0-7407-5835-5
ISBN-10: 0-7407-5835-7

www.andrewsmcmeel.com
www.beckykelly.com

POCKET TREASURES™ is a trademark of
River House Media, Inc.
POCKET TREASURES™ are produced by Jean Lowe,
River House Media, Inc., Leawood, Kansas

Design by Delsie Chambon

Fairy Wishes for Friends

A Pocket Treasure Book
of Friendly Thoughts

Illustrated by Becky Kelly

**Andrews McMeel
Publishing**

Kansas City

With a sprinkle
of stars, and a
flutter of wings,

fairy friends
wish you such
wonderful things.

B. Kelly

Like . . .
the sun on
your face,

and the wind
in your hair,

fields filled with flowers, with plenty to share.

The grass so soft,
wherever
you roam,

and a moonlit path
to guide you
back home.

Arms to
    enfold you,

bright stars
overhead,

and sweet dreams
to hold you, with
the clouds for a bed.

Lighthearted laughter
to guide you along,

as the forest rejoices
in friendship's
sweet song.

With the magic of
fairy dust and your
very own wings,

your fairy friends
wish you these
wonderful things.

B. Kelly